I0447786

The Surname Hulme

Susan Morris &
Wendy Bosberry-Scott

Copyright © 2016 Debrett Ancestry Research Ltd

All rights reserved.

ISBN: 154048260X
ISBN-13: 978-1540482600

The question of surnames, their origins, distribution and history, lies at the heart of genealogy as well as being fascinating in its own right.

In the 1980s and 1990s, long before many genealogical sources were even indexed, let alone online, our Surname Report service provided expert assessments of the origins, history and distribution of selected British surnames, using the sources available at the time.

Now, with so many more sources available, we believe that these reports retain their value as studies of individual surnames, and so we are gradually making the Debrett Surname Archive available online and in print for the first time. Some modern indexes have been consulted to refresh and update the reports.

Debrett Ancestry Research Ltd, PO Box 379,
Winchester SO23 9YQ
Tel: 01962 841904
Email: info@debrettancestry.co.uk
Website: www.debrettancestry.co.uk

CONTENTS

Overview

The use of surnames in England began in the Norman period, when surnames were not necessarily hereditary but usually a form of description. Some described the individual's trade or profession; others were nicknames; some gave the father's Christian name; others gave the individual's place of residence or origin.

Different surnames might be used in different documents, or more than one surname given in one document. Early descriptions were fairly elaborate and by the thirteenth and fourteenth centuries these were simpler, but still variable, and indeed the instability of surnames continued until well into the seventeenth century.

Although some Normans would already have had hereditary surnames on their arrival in Britain, the passing on of a surname from generation to generation only became customary in Britain gradually during the course of the thirteenth and fourteenth centuries. At the end of this period most of the population apparently had surnames.

Variations in the spelling of a family's surname continue to be found until the present century. Before this, as most people could not read or write, the parish clerk or other official would write down the name as they heard it.

There are four main groups of surnames:

> A – Local names, which describe a person by his place of residence or origin.

> B – Occupational names, which describe a person by his trade or profession.

> C – Surnames of relationship, which refer to the Christian name of the father or other important relative.

> D – Nicknames or sobriquets, coined to describe a person in terms of his appearance or character.

Many surnames have uncertain origins, but the name Hulme clearly falls into Category A.

Origins and early examples

The surname Hulme is one of the many English surnames deriving from a place-name and there are several place-names to choose from: Cheadle Hulme, Hulme Walfield or Church Hulme in Cheshire; Hulme or Hulme Hall in Manchester; Hulme in Winwick, Lancashire; or Hulme in Staffordshire. The original bearer of the surname would have been someone who lived or worked in a place called Hulme or who had moved from there.

The source of the place-names is the Old Danish word *hulm* (which corresponds with the Old Norse *holmr*) meaning 'small island' or 'piece of land in a stream'. The word was brought to England by Scandinavian settlers in the ninth century and although the majority of settlers in Cheshire and Lancashire were from Norway, the specific form *hulm* indicates Danish rather than Norwegian origin. There has been very little change in the form of the place-name since its earliest history.

Eilert Ekwall's *Concise Oxford Dictionary of English Place-Names* (4th edition, 1960) lists early forms of particular place-names and these are often a valuable clue to surname origins. Cheadle Hulme is found in documents from 1363 as *Hulm* and in 1528 as *Chedulholme*. Church Hulme was noted as *Churche Hulme* in 1292. Hulme Walford was found in 1290 as *Walefed/Wallefelde Hulm*; in 1308 as *Hulm juxta Wallefeld* and as *Hulm* in 1338.

Ekwall noted the Lancashire place name of Hulme appearing as follows: Hulme near Manchester was found as *Hulm* in 1246 and *Overhulm* and *Netherhulm* in 1324. Hulme near Winwick was shown as *Hulm* in the Lancashire Assizes of 1246 and 1276. Hulme in Staffordshire was found in deeds in 1227 as *Hulm* and in the Staffordshire Assizes as *Holm under Kevermund*.

The surname Hulme has been linked with Home(s) and Holm(e)(s). Holmes has a separate origin but the two names may well have become confused in some families. In his *Dictionary of English Surnames*, (updated by R M Wilson) the late P H Reaney derives the surname Holm(e)(s) from the Old Norse word *holmr* (as opposed to the Danish *hulm*) 'from residence near a piece of flat land in a fen or by a piece of land partly surrounded by streams'; this indicates a topographical rather than a place-name origin. The word *holm* eventually became an Old English word with this meaning. However, Holme does survive as a place-name in many parts of the country such as Bedfordshire, Cumbria, Lancashire, Lincolnshire, Norfolk and Yorkshire; and in several instances cited by Eilert Ekwall *(ibid)* there are examples of these place-names appearing as Hulme in medieval records. For example, Home near Brampton in Derbyshire appears as Hulme in a feet of fine dated 1258.

The distinction between the place-names Holme and Hulme is thus not a clear one and the surname Hulme could have derived from one of the place-names now known as Holme.

To confuse the issue further, some place-names Holme derive not from the Scandinavian word but from the Old English *holegn* meaning 'holly' (this is apparent from their medieval forms). This is true of East and West Holme in Dorset and of Holme near Holmfirth in West Yorkshire. These place-names are thus unlikely to be associated with Hulme surnames.

The surname Hume is clearly related to Hulme and Reaney and Wilson give the following early examples, all from East Anglia:

1221	Walter de Hulmo/Humo	Curia Regis Rolls, Suffolk
1275	Ralph de la Hume	Hundred Rolls, Norfolk
1275	Walter Hume	Hundred Rolls, Suffolk

The surname Hulme has also been found as Hulm and Hulmes and for the purposes of this report we have restricted our research to these three names.

Reaney and Wilson give the following early examples of Hulme:

1169	Turstinus de Hulmo	Pipe Rolls, Huntingdonshire
1202	Geoffrey de Hulm	Lancashire Pipe Rolls
1260	John de Hulm	Cheshire Assizes

To this list can be added a reference from Burke's *General Armory* of 1884, which is of less certain authenticity:

1066-87

Michael Hulme, brother to Walter Hulme, and heir to James Hulme, his nephew, *temp.* William the Conqueror, ancestor of Sir Michael Mannours, Knight 39 Henry III [1254/5]

A collection of London and Middlesex deeds from the medieval period (*A Calendar to the Feet of Fines for London and Middlesex 1189-1485*) provides two further medieval references to Hulme:

Henry VI

John Thoralby, Nicholas Hulme, John de Radclif and Richard de Kellowe, clerks, and John Gybbes, of Oldeforde in the parish of Stebenhith and Alice his wife and John Piers and Rose his wife.
Premises in Stebenhith and Hakeney.
Anno I (1422/23)

Henry VI

Nicholas Hulme, clerk, John de Radclyf, clerk, Richard Kellowe, clerk, and John Richemond of Oldeford and Edith his wife and Thomas Dyse and Joan his wife.
Messuage in Oldeford. Anno 8 (1429/30)

The same man, Nicholas Hulme, clerk (in holy orders), was presumably involved in both of these conveyances.

Distribution

In 1890 H B Guppy published his *Homes of Family Names in Great Britain*, still the only published work on surname distribution in Britain as a whole. His work was based on printed genealogies and a survey of county directories for the 1880s, in which he looked especially at the names of farmers, reasoning that they were among the most stable groups in society. He restricted his study to names that appeared in a proportion of 7:10,000 or higher.

Guppy noted that there was a proportion of forty in ten thousand farmers who used the name Hulme that time in Staffordshire. He also noted that the name appeared in Cheshire (36 in 10,000) and Lancashire (11 in 10,000). These are all counties in which the place-name occurs.

Guppy reasonably assumes that the Cheshire Hulmes take their name from the parish of Hulme in Cheshire. The Hulmes of Hulme date back to the reign of Henry II; the Hulmes of Halsall were Lords of the Manor of Maghull in the sixteenth and seventeenth century; Hulmes were found in Manchester in the reign of Elizabeth I and their family seat was Hulme Hall in Manchester; James Hulme was the Constable of Manchester in 1752; Dauntsey Hulme was a Salford borough reeve in 1797. In Staffordshire, Guppy noted that the name Hulme was centred in the town of Stoke Upon Trent.

The Victorian surname scholar C W Bardsley also did a limited survey of commercial directories during his research *(Dictionary of English and Welsh Surnames, 1901)* and noted that the name Hulme appeared in an 1870 edition of a London directory nine times; in a similar directory for the Manchester area Hulme appeared 34 times and Hulmes appeared twice.

Bardsley also mentions a Henry Hulme of Stockport in 1610 and who appears in an index to Chester wills for the period 1545-1620.

Many of the sources available for charting surname distribution through the centuries are necessarily confined to the wealthier sectors of the population: in general, nobody wanted to know the names of the poor but the names of those with money or land were naturally of interest to the authorities. However, one source that covers the whole of the social spectrum is provided by English parish registers, the earliest of which began in 1538 following a mandate that all parish priests should keep a weekly record of all baptisms, marriages and burials that took place in their parish. A survey of a cross section of parish registers for the years 1601 and 1602 was carried out in 1910 by F K and S Hitching; incidences of a particular surname are noted by parish and county, although with no indication of numbers of references.

In 1601 the name Hulme was found only at Manchester Cathedral, in 1602 it was found again at Manchester Cathedral but also at Didsbury and Leigh (both parishes in Lancashire).

A useful guide to the distribution of surnames for the sixteenth, seventeenth and eighteenth centuries in England is provided by the indexes to wills proved, and administrations granted, at the Prerogative Court of (the Archbishop of) Canterbury, in London, which had superior jurisdiction over local ecclesiastical courts where wills were proved until 1858. The PCC thus provides a national index, although it is not a completely representative one, as testators whose wills were proved in the PCC were mostly among the wealthier members of society, and a disproportionate number of them were from London or Middlesex.

A search of the indexes for the years 1584 to 1800 found numerous entries for testators named Hulme:

1558-1599
1586   Thomas Hulme, gent, London
1591   Thomas Hulme, citizen and haberdasher of Newfishstreete, London
1594   Alice Hulme, widow of Thomas Hulme, haberdasher, London

Seventeenth Century
1619   Anne Hulme, widow of Mathew Hulme, minister and vicar of co Warwick
1619   Matthew Hulme, MA clerke, vicar and parson of Lemington Hastings, Warwickshire
1651   Adam Hulme, Manchester, Lancashire
1653   Robert Hulme, yeoman of Newton, Manchester, Lancashire
1654   Joseph Hulme, citizen and grocer of London
1655   Timothy Hulme of Manchester, Lancashire
1656   William Hulme, husbandman of Kermincham, Cheshire

1656   Margarett Hulme widow of Knifden, Leek, co Staffordshire

1658   John Hulme, yeoman of New Grange, Leek, Staffordshire

1659   William Hulme, grocer of St Lawrence Jury, London

1685   Thomas Hulme, maltster of Frankwell, Shrewsbury, Shropshire

1687   Mary Hulme, widow of London

1692   Richard Hulme, shipwright of Shadwell, Middlesex

Eighteenth Century

1761   Thomas Hulme of Cheshire

1762   William Hulme of Hertfordshire

1763   Thomas Hulme of Huntingdonshire

1764   Ann Hulme of Huntingdonshire

1783   Rebecca Hulme of London

1786   John Hulme of Hertfordshire

1799   William Hulme of Kent

1800-1857

1801   John Hulme, victualler of Sandbach, Cheshire

1804   Humphrey Hulme, gentleman of Flamstead, Hertfordshire

1806   Joseph Hulme, Doctor of Physic of Halifax, Yorkshire

1806   George Hulme of Lombard Street, London

1807   Dr Nathaniel Hulme, MD Physician of Chaterhouse Square, London

1810   William Hulme, wholesale tobacconist of Broad Street Hill, City of London

1810   Robert Hulme of St John Hampstead, Middlesex

1813   Lucy Hulme, widow of Kidderminster, Worcestershire

1813   Samuel Hulme, gentleman of Lambeth Hill, City of London

1817	Susannah Hulme, widow of Hampstead, Middlesex
1818	James Hulme, gentleman of Brunswick Square, Middlesex
1819	Samuel Hulme of Hoxton, Middlesex
1821	Nancy Hulme, widow of Chelsea, Middlesex
1823	Joseph Hulme, gentleman of Pentonville, Middlesex
1825	Samuel Hulme, gentleman late cashier of the Bank of England, of Shoreditch
1826	Zephaniah Hulme, of Islington
1826	Joseph Hulme of Islington, Middlesex
1828	Frances Hulme
1828	Dauntesey Hulme of Salford Lancashire
1830	Alice Hulme, spinster of Walcot, Bath
1830	Jonathan Hulme, surgeon of Ashton upon Mersey, Cheshire
1831	John Hulme, gentleman of Stockport, Cheshire
1832	Arden Hulme of Hampton Wick, Middlesex
1834	Robert Hulme
1836	John Hulme, keeping a house of St Matthew, Bethnal Green, Middlesex
1837	Matthew Hulme, gentleman of St John Westminster, Middlesex
1838	Elizabeth Hulme, widow of Frederick Street, Grays Inn Road, Middlesex
1842	Dr Henry Pritchett Hulme, doctor of medicine of Douglas in the Isle of Man
1843	William Hulme, weaver of Greenhill Rents, Middlesex
1844	James Hulme, yeoman of Alstonefield, Staffordshire
1845	Reverend George Hulme, clerk of Shinfield, Berkshire
1852	Margaret Hulme, widow of Westminster, Middlesex
1852	Betty Hulme, spinster of Ashton upon Mersey, Cheshire

1853   Jane Hulme, widow of Shrewsbury,
        Shropshire
1853   Thomas Hulme, yeoman of West Derby,
        Lancashire
1854   Richard Parrott Hulme of Stoke Gabriel,
        Devon
1854   Elizabeth Hulm, widow of Princes Place,
        Commercial Road, Middlesex
1855   Edward Hulme, gentleman of Tong,
        Shropshire
1855   Mary Hulme, spinster of Cross Street within
        Ashton upon Mersey, Cheshire
1857   James Hulme, victualler of Bow, Middlesex
1857   Sarah Hulme, spinster of Ashton upon
        Mersey, Cheshire

There was only one entry under the name Hulm:
Elizabeth Hulm, a widow of Middlesex, whose will was
proved in 1854. As is usually the case, a high proportion
of testators were locals from the London area, but
Lancashire, Staffordshire and Cheshire (the counties
containing the place name Hulme) are still represented
in significant numbers. References are also found from
two counties adjacent to these three: Warwickshire,
Shropshire. The remaining references are scattered in the
south-east: Kent, Hertfordshire and Huntingdonshire.

For the nineteenth century, H B Guppy's survey has
been mentioned above. Another important Victorian
source is the *Return of Owners of Land of 1873*, sometimes
known as the Modern Domesday Book. This source lists,
county by county, every owner of an acre of land or
more, with their residence (not necessarily the address
of their property) and the acreage of their holding.

Return of Owners of Land

Berkshire	2	Hulme
Chester	15	Hulme
Derbyshire	1	Hulme
Gloucestershire	1	Hulme
Herefordshire	1	Hulme
Lancashire	5	Hulme
	1	Hulmes
Monmouthshire	1	Hulme
Shropshire	2	Hulme
Staffordshire	22	Hulme
Pembroke	1	Hulm

The general pattern shown by the PCC listing is reproduced here, with Cheshire, Lancashire and Staffordshire standing out as the chief counties (confirming Guppy's findings) and a scattering in nearby counties (Derbyshire, Shropshire). The Return also gives a view of what was happening in Wales, where the variant Hulm appears in the far west in Pembrokeshire. Lancashire has the only example of the variant Hulmes.

The first decennial census return in England, Scotland and Wales was taken in 1801, but personal information was only recorded from 1841 onwards. From 1851, the age, occupation and birthplace is given for each member of the household, and so these records provide invaluable genealogical information as well as a fascinating 'snapshot' of the family in the nineteenth century. The latest return currently open to public inspection is that of 1911 and there are now national indexes to the returns from 1841 onwards, although these indexes are not wholly reliable. Using these indexes, we found the following numbers for Hulme, Hulm and Hulmes in England, Scotland and Wales:

6 June 1841
Hulme (3197); Hulmes (268); Hulm (113)

30 March 1851
Hulme (3701); Hulmes (237); Hulm (182)

7 April 1861
Hulme (4617); Hulmes (271); Hulm (94)

2 April 1871
Hulme (5086); Hulmes (378); Hulm (93)

3 April 1881
Hulme (6555); Hulmes (393); Hulm (128)

5 April 1891
Hulme (6616); Hulmes (486); Hulm (110)

31 March 1901
Hulme (7306); Hulmes (490); Hulm (115)

2 April 1911
Hulme (8248); Hulmes (487); Hulm (167)

The fluctuating numbers for the variant Hulm might indicate that the enumerator or indexers might have been inconsistent in recording the name Hulme, however, it is clear that the dominant form of the surname is Hulme, with steadily increasing numbers between 1841 and 1911. The numbers of Hulmes recorded in the census show a steady growth but nowhere near as dramatic as that of Hulme.

Famous bearers of the name

In Debrett's *People of Today* (1996), the following references were found:

> Geoffrey Gordon Hulme CB - civil servant
> John Hulme - writer
> Rev Paul Hulme

The *Dictionary of National Biography* for the British Isles has the following references to people named Hulme:

> Frederick William Hulme (1816-1884) - landscape painter
> Nathaniel Hulme (1732-1807) - physician
> William Hulme (1631-1691) - founder of Hulme's Charity

There are three coats of arms listed in Burke's *General Armory* granted to men of the name Hulme. In *General Armory Two*, published in 1973, there is one further reference to a grant of arms to a Staffordshire Hulme family:

> **Hulme** - (Michael Hulme, brother to Walter Hulme, and heir to James Hulme, his nephew, *temp.* William the Conqueror, ancestor of Sir Michael Mannours, Knight 30 Henry III [1245/46]) Argent six annulets, two, two, and two sable.

> **Hulme** - (Hulme, county Lancashire) Barry of eight or and azure on a canton or, a chaplet gules.

> **Hulme** - (Ball-Hay House, near Leek, Staffordshire) Argent a chevron ermines between three crosses crosslet fitchee sable.

Hulme - (county Staffordshire and London) Barry of six or and sable on a canton argent rose gules. *Crest* A lions head erased argent gorged with a chaplet of roses gules.

Printed Genealogies

The following references have been found to works containing printed genealogies of Hulme families, or genealogies which mention persons bearing the name. The listing emphasises the strongly local nature of the name:

Hulme

Edward Baines Esq. MP, *A History of the County Palatine and Duchy of Lancashire*, (London, 1836) 4 vols, 4to, ii, 394

Rev John Booker MA FSA, *History of the Ancient Chapel of Didsbury of Chorlton in Manchester Parish etc*, (Chetham Society, 1857) fcap, 4to, vol 42, 226, & vol 85, 158

Baines' History of the County of Lancaster, ii, 394

Croston's Edition, ii, 230

Harleian Society, xv, 399; lix, 132; lxiii, 131

The Visitations of Staffordshire, 1614 & 1663-4

William Salt Society, 181

The Visitations of Cheshire, 1613

Staffordshire Pedigrees

J Sleigh, *the History of the Ancient Parish of Leek*, (1883), 2nd edition, 113, 150

M H Miller, *Old Leeke*, (1891), 11, 158

Summary

To conclude, the surname Hulme derives from a place-name of Scandinavian origin, found in Lancashire, Staffordshire and Cheshire, and these three counties constitute the principal home of the surname, although it has been found scattered as widely as Pembrokeshire and Huntingdonshire. Hulme has remained the dominant form although other variants have also survived.

Sources Consulted

P H Reaney, *The Origins of English Surnames* (London: Routledge & Kegan Paul, 1967)

P H Reaney & R M Wilson, *A Dictionary of British Surnames* (Oxford: Oxford University Press, 3rd edition, 1995)

P H Reaney, *A Dictionary of British Surnames* (London: Routledge & Kegan Paul, 2nd edition, 1976)

P Hanks & F Hodges, *A Dictionary of Surnames* (Oxford University Press, 1988)

M A Lower, *Patronymica Brittanica* (London, 1860)

C W Bardsley, *Dictionary of English and Welsh Surnames* (1901: reprinted, Baltimore: Genealogical Publishing Co, 1967)

C L'Estrange Ewen, *Guide to the Origin of British Surnames* (London: John Gifford, 1938)

H B Guppy, *Homes of Family Names in Great Britain* (London, 1890)

Ernest Weekley, *The Romance of Names* (London: John Murray, 2nd edition, 1917)

Ernest Weekley, *Surnames* (London: John Murray, 1917)

George F Black, *The Surnames of Scotland* (New York Public Library, 1946)

Edward McLysaght, *The Surnames of Ireland* (Dublin: Irish University Press, 1977)

T J & Prys Morgan, *Welsh Surnames* (Cardiff: University of Wales Press, 1985)

F K & S Hitching, *References to English Surnames in 1601* (Walton on Thames: Bernau, 1910)

F K & S Hitching, *References to English Surnames in 1602* (Walton on Thames: Bernau, 1911)

Debrett's People of Today (Debrett's Peerage Limited: London, 1996)

The Dictionary of National Biography: Index & Epitome (London, 1906)

The Concise Dictionary of National Biography, Part II, 1901–1950, (Oxford, 1961)

Burke's Family Index (London: Burke's Peerage Limited, 1976)

H R Moulton, *Palaeography, Genealogy & Topography* (Sale Catalogue, 1930)

Prerogative Court of Canterbury Wills (The National Archives: online index)

G W Marshall, *The Genealogist's Guide* (1903; reprinted, Baltimore: GPC 1973)

J B Whitmore, *A Genealogical Guide* (London, 1953)

Charles Bridge, *An Index to Pedigrees* (London, 1867)

Geoffrey B Barrow, *The Genealogist's Guide* (London: Research Publishing Co, 1977)

Sir Bernard Burke, *The General Armory* (London, 1884)

C R Humphrey-Smith ed., *Burke's General Armory Volume II,* (Tabard Press, 1973)

The Return of Owners of Land (1873)

Eilert Ekwall, *The Concise Oxford Dictionary of English Place-Names* (Oxford: Clarendon Press, 4th edition, 1960)

E G Withycombe, *The Oxford Dictionary of English Christian Names* (Oxford: Clarendon Press, 2nd edition, 1950)

W J Hardy & W Page, *A Calendar to the Feet of Fines for London and Middlesex: Vol 1, Richard I – Richard III (1189–1485)* (London, 1892)

Richard McKinley, *The Surnames of Oxfordshire* (English Surnames Series III: Leopard's Head Press, 1977)

Richard McKinley, *The Surnames of Sussex* (English Surnames Series V: Leopard's Head Press, 1988)

Richard McKinley, *The Surnames of Lancashire* (English Surnames Series IV: Leopard's Head Press, 1981)

Richard McKinley, *Norfolk and Suffolk Surnames in the Middle Ages* (English Surnames Series II: Phillimore, 1975)

George Redmonds, *Yorkshire West Riding* (English Surnames Series I: Phillimore, 1973)

Mr Avenell, *The Norman People* (London, 1874)

Debrett's Heraldry (London, 1933)

J P Brooke-Little, revised, *Boutell's Heraldry* (Frederick Warne: London, 1970)

Indexes to 1841–1911 Census Returns of England and Wales (The National Archives/*Ancestry.com*)

www.ingramcontent.com/pod-product-compliance
Lightning Source LLC
Chambersburg PA
CBHW070251290526
45789CB00004B/1825